GET CODING

WITH

DEBUGGING

> How do you make sure your program works?
> Find out with fun puzzles and games!

Kevin Wood

WINDMILL BOOKS

New York

Published in 2018 by **Windmill Books**, An Imprint of Rosen Publishing
29 East 21st Street, New York, NY 10010

Produced for Windmill Books by Alix Wood Books
Designed by Alix Wood
Editor: Eloise Macgregor
Editor for Windmill Books: Kerri O'Donnell

Photo credits: Cover background © Shutterstock; All robot artwork © Adobe Stock Images and Alix Wood;
all other art © Alix Wood

CATALOGING-IN-PUBLICATION DATA

Names: Wood, Kevin.
Title: Get coding with debugging / Kevin Wood.
Description: New York : Windmill Books, 2018. | Series: Computer-free coding | Includes index.
Identifiers: ISBN 9781499482577 (pbk.) | ISBN 9781499482546 (library bound) | ISBN 9781499482461 (6 pack)
Subjects: LCSH: Computer programming--Juvenile literature. | Debugging in computer science--Juvenile literature.
Classification: LCC QA76.6 W66 2018 | DDC 005.1--dc23

Printed in the United States of America
CPSIA compliance information: Batch # BS17WM: For further information contact Gareth Stevens, New York, New York at 1-800-542-2595.

Contents

What Is a Bug?

When the code you write has a problem, we say that it has a "bug." It is actually pretty rare to write a piece of code and for it to work exactly how you want it to the first time. Bugs are just a part of life for a coder! It isn't always the coder's fault. Sometimes the language you are using to write the code has a bug in it!

Debugging is what coders call it when they search through and find any problems in their code. Sometimes a problem can be really obvious the minute you start to look. Other times, the bug can be quite difficult to find.

```
1000100101001000
1101011000101101
0010100011101101
0100101101101100
1110100010110110
0010100101001000
1101011000101101
1000100101001000
0011000110000110
1011101011011010
```

WHY ARE THEY CALLED BUGS?

One story claims that we use the word "bug" to describe these coding problems because a moth was found in an early computer at Harvard University. However, the word was used in **electronics** before that. It may be short for "bugbear" or "bugaboo," which are old words to describe imaginary things that cause fear or concern, such as goblins or spirits.

What do coders do if they find a bug?

They change the code to fix it. Then they test the code to see if their fix worked.

Debugging a piece of code can take time. Sometimes a coder may need to repeat a set of steps over and over, changing little elements each time, until they get the result they want.

GET Programming

How good are you at spotting mistakes? Computers need really clear instructions to know how to do something. They cannot think for themselves. Can you see the mistake in these instructions telling you how to put your shoes and socks on? What should the correct order be?

1. Find shoes

2. Find socks

3. Put on shoes

4. Put on socks

Answers are on page 32

How Do You Write Code?

Before you can work out what went wrong with your code, you need to write some code! So, how do you tell a computer what to do? You need to use a computer language that will translate your commands into something that the computer will understand.

Computers don't understand most words or numbers the way that people do. Computers use a number system known as **binary**. Binary just uses two numbers, 0 and 1. Every command that you give a computer is, at some point, translated into binary. Don't worry though, the language that you use will do this for you!

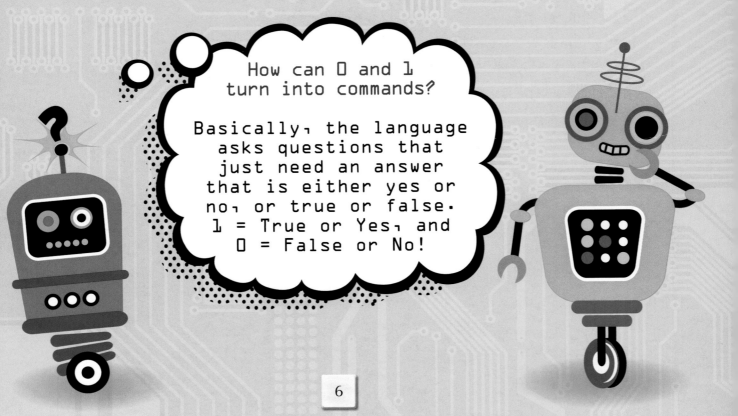

How can 0 and 1 turn into commands?

Basically, the language asks questions that just need an answer that is either yes or no, or true or false. 1 = True or Yes, and 0 = False or No!

GET Programming

Think of a day-to-day task you could program a robot to do for you. Maybe you want him to wash your dishes? Your robot will need to test whether certain **conditions** are true or false. What will you need to ask your robot to get the job done right? Think of all the decisions that you have to make before you put the dishes in the sink!

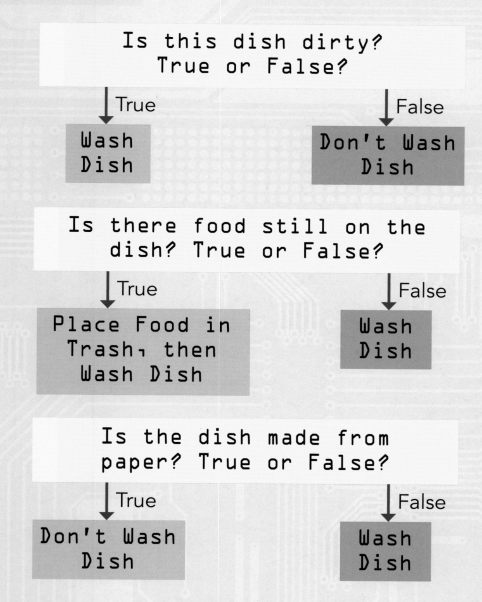

Think of another task you could program a robot to do.
Then try writing it in "True or False" code.

What's Your Language?

There are many different computer languages. Why? Some languages are better for some tasks than others. Some are easier to use than others. Often, the languages that are easy to use are limited in what they can do. Some languages are very powerful and let the coder do almost anything, but they are very hard to learn and to write.

HIGH-LEVEL LANGUAGE

Most languages you use when learning to code are known as high-level languages. Once you are really good at coding you might move on to a low-level language. That sounds backwards! High-level languages are called high-level because of how complex the language itself has to be.

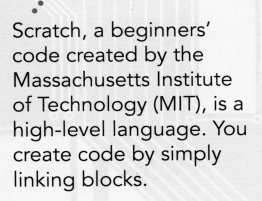

Scratch, a beginners' code created by the Massachusetts Institute of Technology (MIT), is a high-level language. You create code by simply linking blocks.

High-level languages are easy to write. They might allow you to display a picture or a video with just one instruction. The coder has no control over how this is done. Usually this doesn't matter, but it can limit what the coder can do.

LOW-LEVEL LANGUAGE

Low-level languages are much harder to write. To display a picture or video would take many instructions. The result, though, would be much faster and the coder would have full control of every aspect of the code.

```
fib:
    mov edx, [esp+8]
    cmp edx, 0
    ja @f
    mov eax, 0
    ret
```

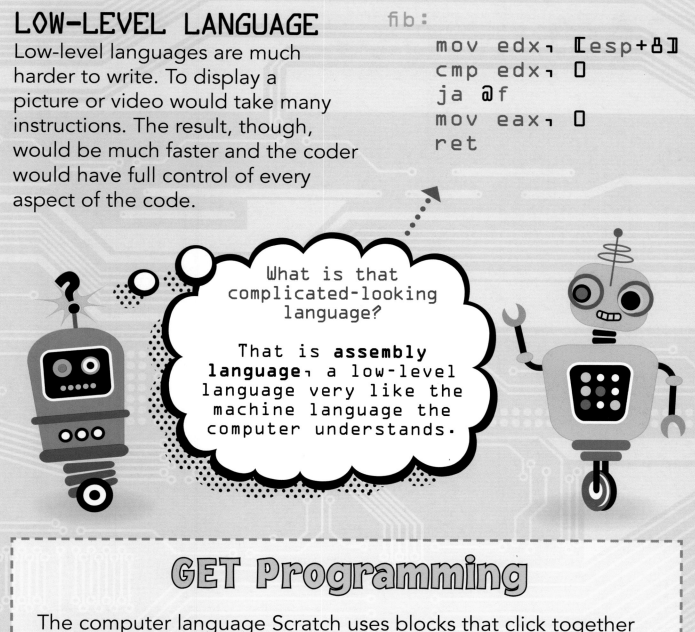

What is that complicated-looking language?

That is **assembly language**, a low-level language very like the machine language the computer understands.

GET Programming

The computer language Scratch uses blocks that click together to make code. It's a neat idea. If you get the order wrong you can easily change the blocks around to get it right. Try making your own code blocks using interlocking toy bricks and sticky notes. Then you can play with the order of your instructions until you get them right.

Find shoes
Find socks
Put on socks
Put on shoes

Try Compiling

The type of language you use affects how you debug your code. Since the computer just understands binary code, the words that you use in your code have to be changed to numbers that the computer can understand. This can be done in different ways. One way is known as **compiling**.

COMPILING

In a low-level language, coders use compilation to turn their code into something the computer can understand. You write your code as normal text and then you compile it into machine-readable code, which is just a long set of numbers. Once this is done, the computer can run or **execute** the code. This is very efficient and very fast. You only compile your code once.

CODING TIPS

Coders who use compilers have to make sure their code doesn't have any bugs before it gets compiled. It's a little like mailing a letter to someone. Once it's been sent, it's gone.

How does a computer change the words we type into numbers it understands? It uses **ASCII**, which stands for American Standard Code for Information Interchange. Each letter and symbol is given an ASCII number. That number is then translated into a 7-**bit** binary number, made up of 0s and 1s.

GET Programming

Be a compiler! Look at the ASCII numbers chart on the right. Each letter has a code number. Can you compile these words into computer friendly ASCII numbers? Separate each number using a "," so you can tell where each one stops and starts. "79, 75"

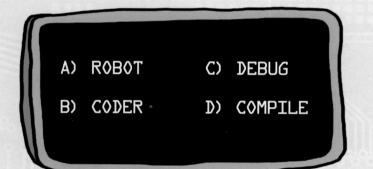

A) ROBOT   C) DEBUG

B) CODER   D) COMPILE

65=A	78=N
66=B	79=O
67=C	80=P
68=D	81=Q
69=E	82=R
70=F	83=S
71=G	84=T
72=H	85=U
73=I	86=V
74=J	87=W
75=K	88=X
76=L	89=Y
77=M	90=Z

Answers are on page 32

> What about lowercase letters such as "a"?
>
> Lowercase and uppercase letters have different ASCII numbers, so the computer knows which one has been used.

Using Interpreters

Most languages use an **interpreter** to turn the code you type into machine-readable code. You may have heard the word "interpreter" to mean someone who **translates** a spoken language into another language.

If you translated something a friend was saying in English into Spanish, you would do it one sentence at a time. If you didn't it would be difficult to remember everything that was said. In coding, interpreters do the same. Interpreters look at your code, one instruction at a time, and convert it into machine-readable code.

> Cinco pequeñas ranitas con lunares sentadas en un tronco de lunares comiendo los más deliciosos bichitos. Yum, yum!
> Uno saltó al agua donde estaba lindo y refrescante. Ahora sólo hay cuatro ranitas con lunares.

CODING TIPS

Interpreting code is slower than running compiled code. It **analyzes** each statement in the program each time it is run and then performs the action. Compiled code just performs the action.

BE AN INTERPRETER

It's hard to guess what the yellow robot on page 12 is saying if you don't know Spanish. It is a lot of words to translate! But what about if you broke it down like an interpreter would? Here are some words that may help you understand it better. Can you guess what it says now? Hint — it's a song.

cinco = five
pequeñas = little
lunares = speckles
ranitas = frogs
bichitos = bugs
refrescante = cool
cuatro = four

Answers are on page 32

GET Programming

Interpreted code shows an error as soon as it comes across one, so it is easier to debug than compiled code. The same song, below, has a typing mistake, but with so many words, can you find it?

Cinco pequeñas ranitas can lunares sentadas en un tronco de lunares comiendo los más deliciosos bichitos. Yum, yum! Uno saltó al agua donde estaba lindo y refrescante. Ahora sólo hay cuatro ranitas con lunares.

It's easier if you just have a small chunk of code to investigate.

The code should say: Cinco pequeñas ranitas con lunares

But the code says: Cinco pequeñas ranitas can lunares

Answers are on page 32

Debugging Scripts

Most languages that you would use when you begin to code use scripts as their language. Scripts are blocks of code that you can join together to write your program. You choose which blocks of code you want to use and what order they go in. Languages such as Scratch and Python use scripts.

BLOCKS OF CODE

Clever programmers have already done a lot of the hard work for you by creating code blocks that perform certain functions. These scripts can do things such as move forward, turn in a direction, say things, or play sounds. You can usually do things like choose different sounds from a library, or record your own.

What could possibly go wrong with my code if I use scripts?

Plenty! The order that you put things in or the math that you use to move around can all have bugs!

GET Programming

Help the frog get safely across the pond. He must hop onto the lily pads to keep safe from the Purple Frog Eater. Use a small object, such as a game piece or a coin, to play with. Test the code scripts below. Can you spot a bug? Can you fix the code to let the frog make it safely across?

Start on first lily pad

a) Go 1 space ↖

b) Go 1 space ↖

c) Go 1 space ↗

d) Go 1 space ↑

e) Go 1 space ↘

f) Go 1 space ↗

g) Go 1 space ↑

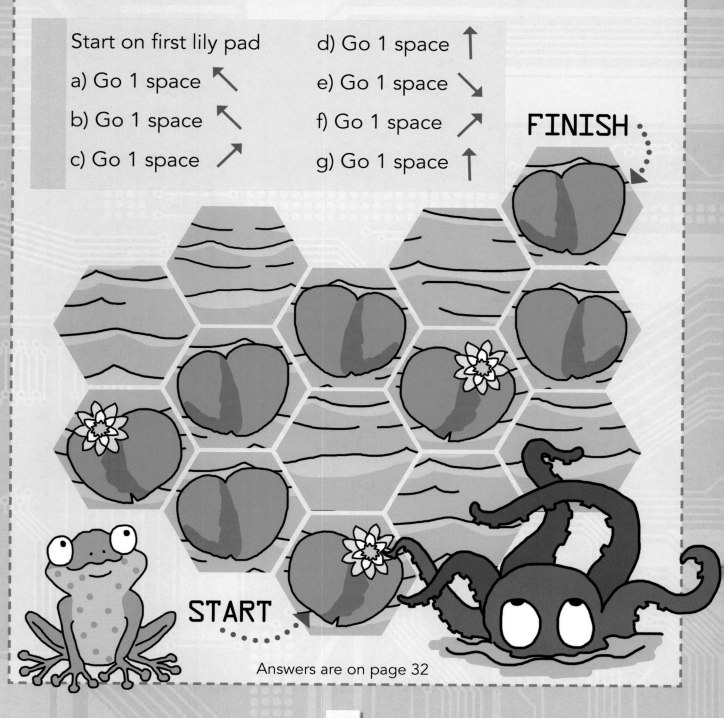

FINISH

START

Answers are on page 32

Syntax Bugs

Syntax is the way commands are written in a computer language. Translators can only run a program if all the words that are used are correct. Syntax bugs might be spelling mistakes, incorrect **punctuation**, or using capital letters in the wrong place.

Why is it so important to get the syntax right?

Computers can't guess what you mean like people can. When you give a computer a command it has to be just right.

PEOPLE POWER

There are some things people are just better at than computers. Guessing what someone means is definitely one of those things! See if you can fill in the missing words in this sentence. I bet you can!

Simon was standing halfway _ _ _ _ _ _ _ the bed and the closet when the _ _ _ _ opened. Simon was so scared. He almost jumped out of his _ _ _ _ !

Answers are on page 32

If a computer gets a command it doesn't understand, it may tell you that it has an error. Even though this can be annoying, it is much better than the computer not realizing that it has been given incorrect code. If the computer runs code which is badly written, all kinds of bad things can happen! This coder mistyped "Go East For Hundred Steps."

100 Steps

...Go East Four Hundred Steps...

Getting the correct syntax isn't easy. Coders need to be able to spell and type without making any mistakes. It's not surprising syntax errors are pretty common!

GET Programming

Here's some code written in a computer language known as Python. Can you see which code below matches it exactly, a or b?

```
print
print "Current date and time using str method
of datetime object:"
print str(now)
```

a)
```
print
print "Current date and time using str method
of datetime object:
print str(now)
```

b)
```
print
print "Current date and time using str method
of datetime object:"
print str(now)
```

Answers are on page 32

Runtime Errors

Runtime errors are errors that you only find when you run the program. These errors cause the program or computer to **crash** even if there appears to be nothing wrong with the program code.

Running out of **memory** will often cause a runtime error. Memory is a computer's temporary storage area. It holds the **data** and instructions that it needs. Sometimes, bugs in code will cause the computer to use up too much memory and the computer will crash.

CODING TIPS

Running certain types of code can make a program crash. An endless loop is a piece of code that continually repeats:

```
:BEGIN
Echo This is an endless
loop!
GOTO BEGIN
```

The program may crash because the loop does nothing and never ends.

> Usually a loop repeats itself until it finds a condition which allows it to stop. Sometimes coders want loops to be endless though. Can you think of a reason why?

Is it just beginners that create runtime errors in their code?

No, sometimes runtime errors are found in code written by professionals. If an error is found, the developers release a **"patch"** or small update that fixes the bug.

GET Programming

Runtime errors sometimes happen if code has been written in the wrong order. When writing code, programmers use these brackets ( ), known as **parentheses**, to show that the thing between them needs to be done first. Coders sometimes get their parentheses in a muddle! Can you work out which part of the problems below needs to be done first? Can you match them to their answer? Note—a * sign means multiply.

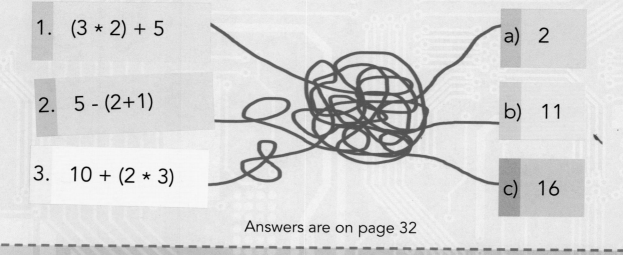

1. (3 * 2) + 5

2. 5 - (2+1)

3. 10 + (2 * 3)

a) 2

b) 11

c) 16

Answers are on page 32

Logical Bugs

Logical bugs can be tricky. These are errors in the coder's thinking. Usually the computer will carry out its instructions with no problem, but it won't do what the coder expected it to. They will have to go through the code carefully to try to find what they might have done wrong.

When you code you often use symbols. Do you know the symbols for less than and greater than?

Less than <
greater than >

We can use these symbols in our code to find values greater than or less than a number.

How do you remember which way the < > symbols go?

5 > 2. Imagine the symbols are hungry alligators. The open mouth faces the largest number.

What happens if we get the symbols muddled? Can you see the problem with our logic here?

If age is > 60 and < 50 give discount

Answers are on page 32

CODING TIPS

Talk your code through with someone else. If no one is around to listen, talk it through with your teddy bear. It may seem silly, but just the process of describing what your code should do to someone else makes the steps clearer in your head!

GET Programming

A logic error might be a sequence that is written in the wrong order, like the shoes and socks on page 5. Sometimes code is given the wrong data. The code might be told to expect a number (4) and it is given a word (four) instead. Code may also contain an incorrect command. Perhaps the code says "If tired, then eat" instead of "If tired and hungry, then eat."

The code below gives instructions on how to draw a square. Can you find any logic bugs? Look hard!

```
                                    b           c

Draw line from a to b
Draw line from B to c
Draw line from c to d
Draw line from d to a

                                    a           d
```

Answers are on page 32

Mistakes Are Normal

```
0010010100100
0101100010110
10001       110
00101    1100
10         0
0          01
00101     1000
11000 10 00110
111010110 1010
```

As you will see, everyone who writes code makes mistakes, even professional coders who have been writing code for years. Debugging is just part of a coder's day. Writing code with errors does not mean you are a bad coder. The trick is in how well you deal with those errors.

ITERATION

The main thing a coder will do to test if their code works is to run it and check it, fixing bugs as they go. This process of repeating steps to improve code is known as **iteration**. Iteration means doing something again and again, usually to improve it.

Each time you run the code you fix any errors. Eventually you will run it and not find any bugs at all.

So, I can still be a good coder and make mistakes?

Yes! Don't ever be afraid to make mistakes. Finding mistakes and fixing them is how you make great code.

EXPECT THE UNEXPECTED!

When you test your code, don't just test for how you expect your code to be used. You also need to be prepared for the unexpected. If you are writing a program that deals with people's ages, what age did you go up to? Are people over 100 accepted in your code? There may not be many people, but your code needs to include them.

Users can do the strangest things, too. What will your code do if someone enters the wrong information? Will it tell them how to do it right, or just fail?

FRIENDLY ERROR MESSAGES

You have set up an online shop. When people buy things from your website, they fill out an order form. They enter their name, address, and payment details. What could go wrong? Plenty! If your customer does something unexpected, what should your code do? Your code gives you the message "FieldT12empty" Do you:

a. Give the customer the message "FieldT12empty" They'll work it out!

b. Translate the message for them, such as "Please enter your zip code"

Answers are on page 32

Program with a Friend

One way to test your code is to get a friend to carry out your instructions. They can be part of your test cycle! Write your code and then run it, by getting your friend to test out your instructions. If anything goes wrong, look back at your code. Repair any mistakes and test it again.

AROUND THE RUG

Try this game with a friend. Find an open space. Place a rug or large sheet of paper on the ground. Label the sides North, South, East, and West. Write some code to direct your friend to walk around the rug without touching it. Don't tell them that this is the goal. That way they can just follow the code without trying to make any adjustments. Only if it is safe to do so, you can ask them to wear a blindfold. Read out your code. If they touch the rug, your code has a bug! Rework the code and try again until it works.

Walk ten paces North.
Walk five step East.
Walk ten paces South.
Walk five step West.

North

West

East

South

GET Programming

The code below tells you how to color in the picture on the squared paper. The arrow keys show you the direction you must move one square. The loop means repeat any command inside the loop by the amount of times written after it. Color in squares the color of the arrow. Start from the square marked • and read each line of code from left to right.

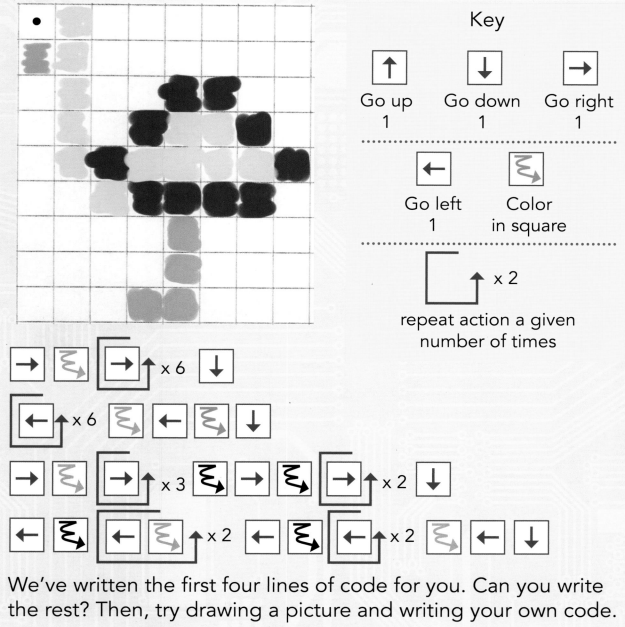

Key

↑	↓	→
Go up 1	Go down 1	Go right 1

←	⧹ (Color in square)
Go left 1	Color in square

⌐↑ x 2

repeat action a given number of times

We've written the first four lines of code for you. Can you write the rest? Then, try drawing a picture and writing your own code.

Answers are on page 32

Documenting Your Code

It is important to make sure the code you write is easy to understand. Other people may want to use it or alter it in the future. You may also forget what some pieces of your code were doing. Errors are easier to fix if the code you are checking through is easy to understand.

HOW TO DOCUMENT CODE

When you write code you want to name everything in a recognizable way. For example, imagine you are writing a program to work out how many cookies are in a pack. You have a **field** where you enter the length of the cookie pack, and a field where you enter the width of an average cookie. You could write your code like this:

```
x = 0.5
y = 170
```

or you could write:

```
AverageCookieWidth = 0.5
CookiePackLength = 170
```

Which one is easiest to understand when you read back your code?

CODING TIPS

The most common way to document your code is by using comments. These are like instructions. In many languages, if you type two slashes (//), anything after the slashes on that line is ignored by the compiler. The coder can write any comments there.

GET Programming

Look at the code that you wrote on page 25. The arrow instructions by themselves are difficult to understand unless you look at the key that tells you what each instruction does.

Can you remember what your code was trying to do? Would you remember in a year's time?

Try to write a new code using the same arrows, but give them different functions. Perhaps they could be instructing a friend to move around the room and then shout out the name of the color? Write your new instructions on a key, so you can always remember what your code was doing.

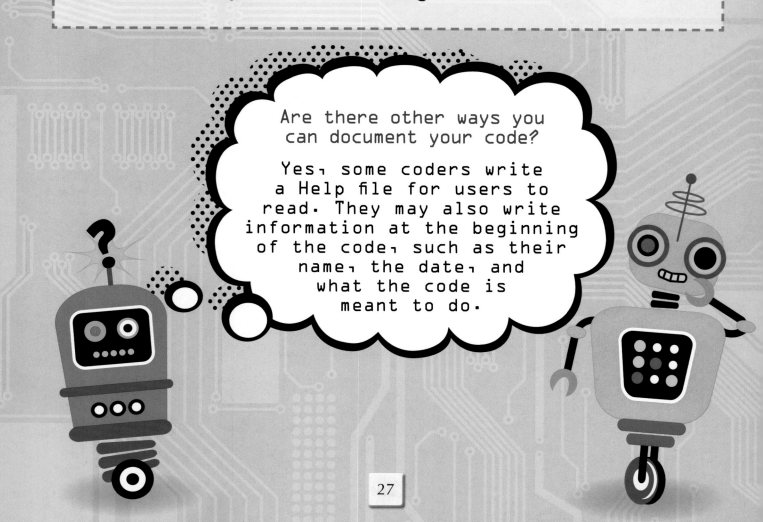

Are there other ways you can document your code?

Yes, some coders write a Help file for users to read. They may also write information at the beginning of the code, such as their name, the date, and what the code is meant to do.

Can You Pass the Test?

1. What is binary?
   a) a number system that uses 0 and 1
   b) the computer's trash can
   c) a computer bug

2. Which level of language is easier to learn?
   a) a high-level language
   b) a low-level language

3. What does ASCII stand for?
   a) Alphabet Sorting Code Is Important
   b) American Standard Code for Information Interchange

4. What letter is 65 in ASCII
   a) A b) B c) C

5. What are Scratch and Python?
   a) zoo animals
   b) computer languages
   c) phone apps

6. A typing mistake is
   a) a syntax bug   b) a logic bug

7. What does it mean if part of a problem is surrounded by parentheses?
   a) Work out that part last
   b) Work out that part first

8. What does this symbol mean >
   a) greater than
   b) less than
   c) equal to

9. What is iteration?
   a) Learning about IT
   b) Repeating steps to check and improve something

10. What do comments help you do?
    a) Forget what your code does
    b) Remember what your code does

11. What is a bug?
    a) a problem with some code
    b) a speck of dirt on a computer screen

Turn this page upside down to see the answers.

Quiz Answers

1. a) a number system that uses 0 and 1; 2. a) a high-level language; 3. b) American Standard Code for Information Interchange; 4. a) A; 5. b) computer languages; 6. a) a syntax bug; 7. b) Work out that part first; 8. a) greater than; 9. b) Repeating steps to check and improve something; 10. b) Remember what your code does; 11. a) a problem with some code

Glossary

analyzes Studies or finds out the nature and relationship of the parts by analysis.

ASCII A code for representing characters as numbers.

assembly language A code for programming a computer that is a close approximation of machine language but is more easily understood by humans.

binary A system made up of two parts or things; in coding, a system using just the numbers 0 and 1.

bit A unit of computer information that represents the selection of one of two possible choices.

compiling To translate (as a computer program) with a compiler.

conditions Something essential to the occurrence of something else.

crash To go out of order suddenly.

data Facts about something that can be used in calculating, reasoning, or planning.

electronics A branch of physics that deals with the giving off, action, and effects of electrons and with electronic devices.

execute To put into effect.

field In computers, a field is a space that holds specific parts of data from a set or a record.

interpreter A computer program that translates an instruction into machine language and executes it before going to the next instruction.

iteration A computational process in which a series of operations is repeated a number of times.

memory The capacity for storing information.

parentheses A pair of curved marks used to enclose something ( ).

patch A piece of software designed to update a computer program or its supporting data, to fix or improve it.

punctuation Marks in written matter that make the meaning clear and separate the parts.

translates To change from one language into another.

BOOKS

Harris, Patricia. *Understanding Coding with Scratch (Spotlight on Kids Can Code)*. New York, NY: PowerKids Press, 2016.

Saujani, Reshma. *Girls Who Code: Learn to Code and Change the World*. New York, NY: Viking Books, 2017.

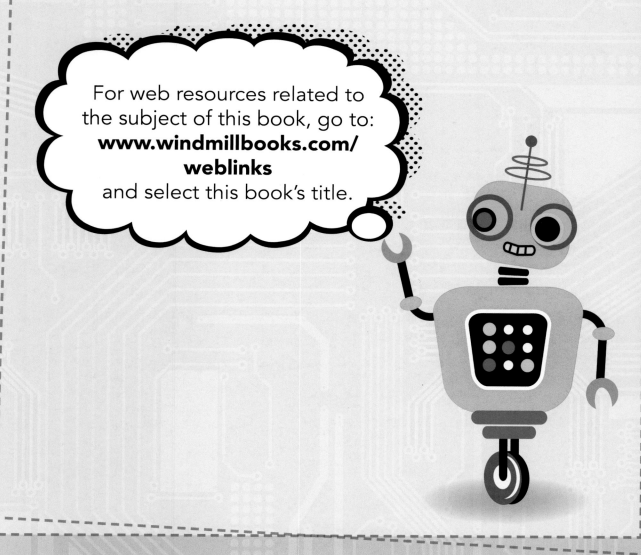

For web resources related to the subject of this book, go to: **www.windmillbooks.com/ weblinks** and select this book's title.

Index

• •

Answers

page 5: correct order 1, 2, 4, 3

page 11: a) 82, 79, 66, 79, 84, b) 67, 79, 68, 69, 82, c) 68, 69, 66, 85, 71, d) 67, 79, 77, 80, 73, 76, 69

page 13 top: Five little speckled frogs sat on a speckled log, eating the most delicious bugs. Yum, yum! One jumped into the pool, where it was nice and cool. Now there are four speckled frogs.

page 13 bottom: "con" is written "can"

page 15: d is wrong, should be ↗

page 16: between, door, skin

page 17: b

page 19: 1) 3 * 2 (b), 2) 2+1 (a), 3) 2 * 3 (c)

page 20: no one can be older than 60 and younger than 50

page 21: "B" should be "b"

page 23: b

page 25:

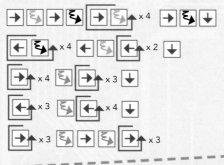